THIS CANDLEWICK BOOK BELONGS TO:

_____

_____

_____

For Wendy and Matthew

This U.S. paperback edition 2011

The Library of Congress has cataloged the hardcover edition as follows:

Williams, Marcia.
Greek myths for young children / Marcia Williams —1st U.S. ed.
Summary: Retells eight Greek myths in a comic-strip format, including "Pandora's Box," "The Twelve Tasks of Heracles," and "Theseus and the Minotaur."
ISBN 978-1-56402-115-1 (hardcover)
1. Mythology, Greek—Caricatures and cartoons—Juvenile literature.
[1. Mythology, Greek—Cartoons and comics. 2. Cartoons and comics.]
I. Title
BL782.W56   1992
398.2'0983—dc20
ISBN 978-0-7636-5384-2 (paperback)

18 19 20 APS 10 9 8 7

Printed in Humen, Dongguan, China

This book was typeset in Monotype Centaur and Truesdell.
The illustrations were done in watercolor and ink.

Candlewick Press
99 Dover Street
Somerville, Massachusetts 02144

visit us at www.candlewick.com

GREEK MYTHS

RETOLD AND ILLUSTRATED BY

by MARCIA WILLIAMS

CANDLEWICK PRESS

Prometheus then offered both sacks to Zeus.

Zeus chose the one with steak on top,

but when he discovered the true contents, he roared with anger.

In revenge, Zeus extinguished every spark of fire on earth,

leaving people cold and hungry.

But Prometheus did not want his beloved humans to suffer.

So he stole up Mount Olympus and broke off a blazing piece of sun for the people.

For this, Zeus punished Prometheus by chaining him to a rock.

Each day a great vulture tore out his liver. And each night, his liver grew again. The torture continued for months before Prometheus was released.

Zeus also punished humans. He ordered the gods to create a beautiful woman.

Her name was Pandora and she was to be married to Prometheus's brother.

Epimetheus, fearful of Zeus, married Pandora at once.

Pandora was vain and self-centered.

She nagged her husband constantly.

She demanded he open a special, locked box. Epimetheus refused,

as Prometheus had entrusted the box to his care.

In that box was trapped every known evil and disease.

But her husband's stubbornness made Pandora more determined.

Convinced that the box held jewels, she planned to steal it.

One day, while Epimetheus slept,

Pandora stole the box and its key.

Eagerly, she fit the key into the lock.

It turned, and she lifted the lid . . .

All at once, every evil and spite flew out, like a swarm of insects, covering Pandora and infesting the earth with pain and sorrow.

Luckily, Prometheus had also locked "hope" in the box, so people were saved from total despair. But, thanks to Pandora, life on earth was never quite so joyful again.

ARION AND THE DOLPHINS

Like most Greeks, Periander, King of Corinth, was a music lover.

His court was crowded with singers and musicians.

But his favorite star was Arion. Arion's music always put Periander in a good mood.

So when Arion asked to visit Sicily for a music festival, Periander hated the idea.

"I shall be grouchy all the time you are away," he declared gloomily.

Finally, Arion convinced him that it would be worth all the prize money he would win.

So a ship was rigged and manned, and Arion set sail for Sicily.

Once there, it seemed that Arion could not play or sing a wrong note.

He won so many prizes that it took twelve porters to carry them to the ship.

Arion was delighted to be returning home to Periander with such fame and fortune.

The sailors were delighted too, for they were thinking of stealing the prizes.

When the ship was well out to sea, they surrounded Arion with shouts of, "You must die!"

Arion tried to persuade them to take his gold and spare his life.

But the sailors felt they would only be safe with Arion dead.

Arion pleaded to be allowed to sing one last song.

He knelt on the prow and sang to the gods to look on him kindly.

Then, as the last notes died away, he threw himself into the sea.

The waves closed over him and the ship sailed on.

Arion's beautiful singing attracted a school of dolphins that took him to the shores of Corinth.

Arriving home before the ship, Arion related his adventures to Periander.

Relieved to have Arion back, Periander swore to punish the sailors.

When the sailors returned, Periander hid Arion behind a screen, and then summoned them.

"Have you news of Arion?" Periander asked. "Why, yes," the sailors replied. "He has been delayed in Sicily by all the festivities."

As they spoke these words, Arion appeared from behind the screen.

The sailors tried to run away, but the guards surrounded them.

Periander was all for having the murderous thieves executed on the spot,

but Arion was more merciful and begged for their lives.

So Periander banished them to an ugly, barbarous land.

This done, Periander settled back to enjoy some of Arion's finest singing.

As the music floated around him, Periander's thoughts grew calm and, for the first time since Arion had left, a smile came to his lips.

ORPHEUS AND EURYDICE

Orpheus was a famous poet and musician. People came from all over Greece to hear him play his lyre and sing.

His music made wild beasts tame and trees bend to listen.

Orpheus loved the beautiful nymph, Eurydice. The day they married was the happiest in his life.

Eurydice loved dancing and often went to romp in the fields. But one day, dancing among the the meadow flowers, she stepped on a deadly snake.

The snake sank its poisonous fangs into her ankle. Eurydice, overcome by the fatal poison, died instantly.

Orpheus, when he heard the news, was inconsolable. For days he would neither eat nor drink, and his friends feared for his life.

Then, without a word, he took his lyre and left the house. He traveled to Hades, the land of the dead, to beg for the return of his beloved Eurydice.

At last he came to the River Styx where Charon, the ferryman, waited to carry the dead across to the underworld.

At first Charon refused to take the living Orpheus.

But when Orpheus played to him upon his lyre, Charon relented.

On the other side of the river, Orpheus's journey became a nightmare.

First he had to travel through the asphodel fields —
fields that were dark and gray and haunted by ghosts.

Then on he went through Tartarus, where the evil were tortured and
where the guard dog, Cerberus, growled and snapped at his heels.

Finally, Orpheus reached the world of the dead. He knelt before King Pluto and his queen,
Persephone, who were amazed that a living person should risk his own life to reach their kingdom.

Orpheus then took up his lyre and sang of his love for Eurydice
and of his great sorrow. Pluto and Persephone were moved to tears.

They agreed to release Eurydice, but on one condition:

Orpheus was not to look back until he reached the world of the living.
So Orpheus departed, without knowing whether Eurydice followed or not.

As he came to the River Styx, he hesitated: If Pluto and Persephone
had tricked him, this was his last chance to go back.

With one foot in the boat, Orpheus turned —
and saw his beloved Eurydice, smiling upon him.

But then her living form faded and Eurydice
became a ghost of the underworld.

And as Charon slowly ferried him into the sunlit world, Orpheus
realized that this time he had lost his love forever.

First, Heracles had to kill the lion of Nemea whose hide was so thick that no sword could penetrate it.

Next, he had to kill the many-headed Hydra, whose very breath could kill man or beast.

Third, he had to capture the sacred, golden-horned deer, an animal as swift as the wind.

The fourth task was to catch a savage boar whose tusks could pierce any armor.

Next, Heracles had to clean out the vast and filthy stables of King Augeas in a single night.

Then he had to to destroy a flock of man-eating birds that hid in a dangerous swamp.

The seventh task was to capture the fire-breathing, marauding bull of Crete.

Next, he had to steal Diomedes's horses, which fed on human flesh.

Then Heracles had to fetch the golden girdle worn by the queen of the Amazon warrior women.

The tenth task was to seize the monster Geryon's cattle, guarded by his two-headed dog.

The eleventh, to collect three golden apples protected by a ferocious dragon.

Heracles's twelfth and last task was the most dangerous of all: to fetch the three-headed guard dog, Cerberus, from Hades itself.

His twelve tasks completed, Heracles returned to King Eurystheus.

The king was dismayed to see him alive, and quickly sent him packing.

Then, to avoid angering the gods, Heracles sent Cerberus back to Hades.

At the temple, Heracles was finally pardoned.

He was content at last, and stronger than ever!

And Hera never bothered Heracles again.

But Daedalus hit on a clever plan — he and Icarus would fly like birds away from Crete.

Using feathers bound with wax and twine, he made them both a pair of wonderful wings.

As he fixed Icarus's wings to his back, Daedalus warned his son:

"Do not fly too close to the sea or your wings will get wet,

nor too close to the sun, or the wax will melt."

Then Daedalus and Icarus rose into the air and flew away.

People below were amazed. They thought they must be seeing gods.

At first Icarus stayed close behind his father,

but soon he was overwhelmed with the joy of flying.

Higher and higher he rose,

closer and closer to the sun . . .

until its
hot brilliance
surrounded him.

Then, suddenly, Icarus felt the wax melt. He saw feathers floating all around him.

His arms would not hold up the air and he plunged toward the sea.

Stop playing games, Icarus!

Icarus, where are you?

Meanwhile, Daedalus had lost sight of his son.

He saw nothing but a few feathers floating on the waves.

He hovered over the sea until Icarus's body floated to the surface.

Weeping, Daedalus carried his dead son to an island,

where he gently laid the body in a grave.

As Daedalus smoothed the earth, a partridge landed beside him.

Daedalus believed it to be the spirit of his nephew, Talos, and he knew that the gods had at last punished him by allowing Icarus to fall to his death, just as Talos had done.

PERSEUS
AND THE GORGON'S HEAD

King Acrisius of Argos was a worried man.

He had been warned that his daughter, Danaë, would have a son who would kill him.

So when Danaë bore a baby boy, named Perseus,

Acrisius put them both in a wooden chest

and pushed it out to sea.

For days the chest tossed on the waves.

Finally, it washed up on the shores of Seriphus

where Dictys, the brother of King Polydectes, found it.

He was amazed to see Danaë and Perseus inside.

The grumpy king allowed them to stay in the palace.

Perseus grew up strong and handsome.

Meanwhile, the king fell in love with Danaë.

He proposed to her at every opportunity.

And at every opportunity, Danaë refused him.

Polydectes plotted to get rid of Perseus by sending him on a deadly mission.

Still Danaë refused to marry the king.

So Polydectes sent Perseus to fetch the head of the Gorgon Medusa.

Medusa was one of three monstrous sisters, with brass hands and golden wings, whose glance could turn men and beasts to stone.

But Perseus was not afraid.

He traveled for many days

but found no sign of Medusa.

Wearily, he lay down to rest.

As he slept, the goddess Athena came to him, bringing him a shield

in which he could look at Medusa's reflection, so that he would not be turned to stone.

The next day he set off again, but there was still no sign of Medusa.

That night, the god Hermes visited Perseus.

He gave him a sickle with which to cut off Medusa's snake-covered head.

Then Hermes told Perseus to go to the Gray Ones.

These three sisters had only one eye and one tooth between them.

Perseus went to Mount Atlas, where the Gray Ones lived.

Creeping up behind them, he snatched their single eye and tooth.

The Gray Ones screamed for them to be returned

and Perseus agreed, in exchange for information.

So they told him he should seek out the Ocean Nymphs.

Then Perseus returned the eye and tooth and went on.

Upon reaching the ocean, he called to the Nymphs.

They hated Medusa and were glad to assist Perseus.

They gave him winged sandals, so he could fly,

a helmet to make him completely invisible,

and a bag in which to put Medusa's deadly head.

Then they directed him to where the Gorgons lived.

There, Perseus heard their rumbling, growling snores.

Looking into his shield, he beheld a fearful sight.

But, fearlessly, Perseus raised his sickle high . . .

and with one mighty stroke, sliced off Medusa's head.

In a moment, he had it in the bag.

As he leapt into the air, Medusa's sisters woke.

Quickly, Perseus donned the helmet and instantly vanished from their sight.

His journey home was not an easy one.

But, after a year, he arrived at Seriphus.

Perseus found his mother hiding from King Polydectes in the temple.

So he went on to the palace.

Polydectes was convinced that Perseus had long since been turned to stone.

The king was horrified to see him alive.

But before he could speak, Perseus pulled out Medusa's head.

Its gaze immediately turned the king to stone.

Perseus then rescued his mother and, before leaving the island, crowned Dictys the new King of Seriphus.

They sailed for Argos where, later, Perseus accidentally killed King Acrisius, as the oracle had predicted.

THESEUS AND THE MINOTAUR

King Minos of Crete had long hated the people of Athens,

for they had killed his son when he took all the prizes at the Athenian games.

To prevent King Minos from waging war against them,

every nine years the Athenians sent seven youths and maidens to be sacrificed to

the Minotaur — half-man, half-bull — that lived in the Labyrinth on Crete.

Theseus, son of King Aegeus, was angered by this cruelty.

Bravely, he offered to join the next victims and try to kill the Minotaur.

His father begged him not to go with the others,

but Theseus insisted, and prepared to sail for Crete.

He hoisted a black sail as a sign of respect for the victims, but promised to return with a white sail raised, as a sign of his success.

Great storms battered the little ship on its journey to Crete.

When Theseus finally landed, he found King Minos waiting with his daughter Ariadne.

Ariadne immediately fell madly in love with Theseus,

and she resolved to save him from the Minotaur and marry him.

That night, Ariadne crept softly past the guards.

She gave Theseus a sword, and a ball of magic thread to guide him out of the maze.

Next day, the Athenians were thrown into the Labyrinth.

Once inside, Theseus tied one end of the thread to the door and set off in search of the Minotaur.

The Labyrinth was a confusing maze of cold, dark passages.

Some led nowhere.

Others took him deeper into the maze.

The roar of the Minotaur grew louder.

ROAR!

Suddenly Theseus came face to face with the hideous monster.

The struggle was long and fierce, for the Minotaur was enormously strong.

But Theseus eventually drove his sword through its heart and it sank to the ground, dead.

Following the thread, Theseus traced his path back to the entrance of the Labyrinth.

Hearing the cheers of Theseus's friends, Ariadne quickly unlocked the door.

Then everyone ran for the ship and set sail for Athens.

After a few days, they stopped at an island, where Ariadne fell asleep.

Theseus, unwilling to marry his enemy's daughter, left her sleeping on the sand.

In all this excitement, Theseus forgot to change his sail from black to white.

Meanwhile, his father, King Aegeus, watched anxiously for his ship.

Sighting the black sail and thinking the worst, he threw himself onto the rocks below.

As Athenian parents celebrated their children's return, Theseus mourned the death of his father.

So the sad but heroic Theseus became King of Athens and lived to win many more victories.

ARACHNE VERSUS ATHENA

Arachne lived with her father in a poor Greek village.

She was not a very beautiful girl, or a very nice one.

But she was an excellent weaver, probably better than anyone else in Greece.

Arachne certainly thought so, and never tired of telling others.

Many people thought that her skill must have been learned from the great goddess Athena.

But the arrogant Arachne denied this, believing that she was even cleverer than the goddess.

This boasting was unwise, for the gods were quick to anger when humans claimed great powers.

Morning, noon, and night, Arachne's father begged her not to compare herself to Athena.

But nothing checked Arachne's conceited tongue. She even challenged Athena to a weaving contest.

Soon afterward, an ugly old woman came to Arachne.

She told Arachne to withdraw her challenge to Athena.

Arachne laughed, declaring that she could out-weave anyone.

The old woman quivered from head to toe with rage, until suddenly . . .

she was transformed into her true self— the all-powerful goddess Athena.

Even then the foolish Arachne was unafraid. Athena decided, therefore, to teach her a lesson.

So two looms were set side by side, and the amazing contest began.

All day the shuttles flashed back and forth, weaving designs in marvelous colors.

Athena's cloth depicted the gods in all their glory.

But Arachne's cloth showed the gods as drunken fools.

When the sun went down and the last threads had been woven, the contest ended.

Athena turned to look at Arachne's work.

It was indeed quite perfect, almost as perfect as her own.

But when Athena saw Arachne's insult to the gods, she exploded.

Taking up her shuttle, she slashed Arachne's cloth in two.

Then, turning on Arachne, she beat her on the head.

Even Arachne was awed by such fury. Fearing an even worse fate,

she tied a noose around her neck and hanged herself from a beam.

There she swayed, the life slowly being squeezed out of her body.

Arachne's father, horrified at her plight, begged Athena to spare his daughter.

Grudgingly, the goddess agreed to let her rival live.

She sprinkled herbs upon Arachne — and there began a dreadful transformation.

First, Arachne's hair fell out.

Then her nose, ears, and legs fell off.

Her arms disappeared so that her fingers cleaved to her sides.

Her head and body shrank until she was no bigger than a fist.

And finally, the rope by which Arachne dangled became a fine, silken thread.

Athena had taken her revenge — she had turned the boastful Arachne into a spider!

Marcia Williams spent a year creating the artwork for *Greek Myths*, often working for a week on a single page. "The decorative detail takes ages," she explains. "I also tried to give each story a character all its own with its own color theme so that each seemed contained. This is important in a collection." Marcia Williams has written and illustrated many books for children, including *Tales from Shakespeare, More Tales from Shakespeare, Charles Dickens and Friends*, and *Archie's War*.